OINK!
THE PIG JOKE BOOK

by

Sandy Ransford

Illustrations by Andy Hammond

0233995706 4 502 F3

LEICESTER LIBRARIES AND INFORMATION SERVICES	
02339957064502	
PETERS	30-Jul-99
J	£3.50

First published in Great Britain in 1999 by Madcap Books,
André Deutsch Ltd, 76 Dean Street, London, W1V 5HA
www.vci.co.uk

Text copyright © 1999 Madcap Books
Illustrations copyright © 1999 Madcap Books

Cover illustration by Andy Hammond
Cover design by Don MacPherson

A catalogue record for this title is available from
the British Library

ISBN 0 233 99570 6

All right reserved. This book is sold subject to the condition that it
may not be reproduced, stored in a retrieval system, or transmitted,
in any form or by any means, electronic, mechanical, photocopying,
recording or otherwise, without the publisher's prior consent.

Typeset by Design 23
Printed in Great Britain

INTRODUCTION

We all love to laugh at pigs. Round, fat and pink, with funny little eyes, curly tails and a distinctive air about them, they are wonderfully comic, whether rootling around in the mud, going 'oink, oink', or squealing with excitement. And their piglets are so delicate and pretty, they remind us of human babies. But although we make jokes about them, we shouldn't underestimate them. Pigs are much misunderstood. Because they roll in mud to protect their skins, we think of them as dirty, whereas they are very clean in their habits. A pig, unlike a cow or a sheep, never soils its house if it can go outside. Pigs are also very intelligent, and will make friends with you, given the chance. I knew someone who had a pet pig that used to come into the house and sit by the fire with the dog on winters' nights. It always behaved perfectly, and made less mess with muddy feet than the dog did! So while you are having a good laugh at the hundreds of different pig jokes in this book, remember that pigs have feelings, too, and try not to insult any you may meet. Just tell them the kinder jokes, and see if they laugh with you. OINK, OINK!

Sandy Ransford

What did the first pig
say to the second pig?
'Let's be pen-pals.'

What do you get
from a pig
with fleas?
Pork scratchings.

What has four trotters, a curly tail and goes KNIO, KNIO?
A pig walking backwards.

What has eight trotters, two curly tails and
goes ʞNIO 'ʞNIO ?
Two pigs in Australia.

Why are piglets so greedy?
They want to make hogs of themselves.

PIGS
RULE

How do you fatten a porker?
Throw him over a cliff and
he'll come down plump.

Which play did Shakespeare write for baby pigs?
Hamlet.

FARMER: Can you cure the fleas on my pig?
VET: Possibly. What's wrong with them?

FARMER: Can you cure my pig's pimples?
VET: I never make rash promises.

What can you put
on a pig's pimples?
Oinkment.

How do you make a pig stew?
Keep him waiting a few hours.

ANDY: What's fat, pink, smelly and made of cement?
MANDY: I don't know. What is fat, pink, smelly and made of cement?
ANDY: A pig.
MANDY: But what about the cement?
ANDY: I just threw that in to make it hard.

What's fat, pink, smelly and blue in the face?
A pig holding its breath.

Why did the pig hold its breath?
It couldn't stand its smell.

How do you keep a pig
in suspense?
Tell you next week.

Where do the cleanest pigs live?
Bath.

Why can't a pig's nose be 12 inches long?
Because if it were it would be a foot.

What do you call a pig without ears?
Anything you like because it can't hear you.

Where do you find black pigs?
It depends where you leave them.

What's pink,
round and smells?
A pig's bum.

What are the little white things in a pig's head that bite?
Teeth.

JENNY: Our pig is just like a member of the family.
KENNY: Really? Who?

How do you keep a pig from smelling?
Put a clothes peg on its nose.

What's the difference between a pig and a dog?
A pig uses a cheaper deodorant.

What do you get if you cross a pig with an owl?
A creature that smells and doesn't give a hoot.

What do you get if you cross a pig with a salmon?
Dirty and wet.

What do you get if you cross a pig with a bee?
Something that stinks and stings.

What do you get if you cross a pig with a porcupine?
A pongy pincushion.

What do you get if you cross a pig with a bear?
Winnie the Pooh.

What do you get if you cross a pig with Richard
Branson's balloon?
A creature that stinks to high heaven.

How do you keep flies
out of the kitchen?
Keep a couple of pigs
in the dining-room.

How do you do a sculpture of a pig?
You get a large piece of wood and then carve away
anything that doesn't look like a pig.

Who wrote *Living With Pigs in the House*?
I. Malone.

BILL: Why did you come home early from your farm
holiday?
GILL: Well, the first day a pig died and we had roast pork
for dinner. The second day a cow died and we had roast
beef for dinner. The third day the farmer died . . . .

DAD: Why are you cross, Bertie?
BERTIE: Because Harry was rude about you. He said
you were not fit to live with pigs.
DAD: And what did you say to him?
BERTIE: I stood up for you. I said of course you were.

What's pink and white
and travels at 100 mph?
A train driver's ham
sandwich.

Gerry was out walking a pet piglet when he met Terry.
'Hey,' said Terry, 'how come you've got a pet piglet?'
   'Oh,' said Gerry, 'I got her for my sister.'
   'Great!' said Terry. 'I wish I could do a swap like that!'

JANE: What's the difference between pig manure and chocolate?
WAYNE: I don't know.
JANE: Then I'm not sending you out to buy any chocolate!

What's the difference between a pig and a biscuit? You can't dip a pig in your tea.

Why are pigs' trotters like ancient tales?
They're both leg-ends.

Why did the pig eat little bits of metal all day?
It was his staple diet.

JOHN: I bet I can get you to forget about pigs.

DON: What pigs?

JOHN: See, you've forgotten already.

EVE: Is it good manners to eat bacon sandwiches with your fingers?

STEVE: No, fingers should be eaten separately.

Where do pigs go when they die?
To the sty in the sky.

What squeals more loudly than a pig at feeding time?
Two pigs at feeding time.

DINER: Do you have pigs' trotters?

WAITER: Yes, sir.

DINER: Well, keep your shoes on and no one will notice.

What do you call
a man who steals pigs?
A hamburglar.

FREDDIE: Look at that flock of pigs.

EDDIE: It's not flock, it's herd.

FREDDIE: Heard what?

EDDIE: Herd of pigs.

FREDDIE: Of course I've heard of pigs.

EDDIE: I mean a pig herd.

FREDDIE: I don't care if a pig heard, I didn't say anything it shouldn't hear.

What do you get if you cross
a pig with a phone?
Crackling on the line.

'Doctor, doctor, can you help me? I keep thinking
I'm a pig.'
'How long has this been going on?'
'Ever since I was a piglet.'

Why is a pig longer in the morning than at night?
Because he's let out every morning and taken in again
at night.

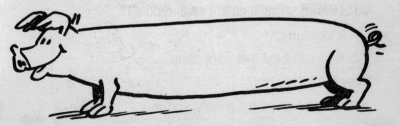

9

What goes 'oink, oink, oink, bang!'?
A pig in a minefield.

Why did the mother pig feed her piglets onions?
So she could find them in the dark.

VISITOR: Are your piglets boys or girls?
FARMER: Of course. What else could they be?

What can't you do if you put three pigs in the fridge?
Shut the door.

CUSTOMER: A pound of pigs' kiddles, please.
BUTCHER: You mean pigs' kidneys.
CUSTOMER: That's what I said, diddle I?

'Waiter, I can't eat this pork chop.'
'Why not?'
'You haven't given me a knife and fork.'

'Waiter, you're not fit to serve a pig!'
'I'm doing my best, sir.'

MERYL: What does your dad do?
CHERYL: He's a sorter on the farm.
MERYL: What sort of sorter?
CHERYL: A sorter pig-keeper.

Why do pink pigs eat more than black pigs?
There are more of them.

When do pigs eat biscuits?
When they're crackers.

Why did the pig stand on her head?
She was turning things over in her mind.

When do pigs have 12 feet?
When there are three of them.

What's fat, pink, goes oink and lights up?
An electric pig.

CAROL: How big is a pig?
DARRYL: What kind of pig?
CAROL: A big one.

How can you tell if there's a pig in your porridge?
It's very lumpy.

Why don't pigs eat Penguins?
They can't take the wrappers off.

Why is a pig like a bottle of ink?
It keeps going into the pen and then running out.

Why are pigs always arguing?
Because they like to raise a stink.

SALLY: I think Susie's new boyfriend is a pigman.
SHEILA: Yes, he does have a certain air about him.

MOTHER PIG: You're pretty dirty, Amelia.
AMELIA PIGLET: I'm even prettier clean.

Where does a very large, bad-tempered pig sit when it goes to the cinema?
Anywhere it wants to.

Mary had a little pig,
It leaped around in hops.
It leaped into the road one day,
And finished up as chops.

FIRST PIG: How's Patricia Pig getting on with her diet?
SECOND PIG: Very well. She's almost disappeared.

MR JONES: I'd like to buy a pig. How much are they?
DEALER: £20 apiece.
MR JONES: How much is a whole one?

Why did the pig scratch itself?
Because no one else knew where it itched.

'That pig is a creature of many parts.'
'Yes, but someone did a terrible assembly job.'

PATTY PIG: Do you think Peter Pig is
bad looking?
PETRA PIG: He might look worse
if I had my glasses on.

'That pig's so huge if he took a
shower his feet would stay dry.'

13

How many pigs does it take to make a big stink?
A phew.

Why is a pig like a bee?
They both hum.

What's fat, pink, smelly and noisy?
A pig playing the drums.

What's fat, pink, goes oink and has red spots?
A pig with measles.

Why did the pig wear a blonde wig?
To see if blondes have more fun.

14

Why did the pig wear a large green hat?
So it could walk across a snooker table without being
seen.

What goes oink and lives under the sea?
A pig with an aqualung.

What smells worse than a pig?
Two pigs.

What's the difference
between school dinners
and a bucket of pigswill?
School dinners come on a plate.

MR GREEN: What are you going to do with that
pig manure?
MR BROWN: Put it on my strawberries.
MR GREEN: Really? I put cream on mine.

What usually runs in a pig's family?
Their noses.

What do you get if you cross a wild pig with a snake?
A boar constrictor.

FIRST PIG: What's your new boyfriend like?
SECOND PIG: Fat, ugly, greedy, smelly – and he has some bad points too.

NELLY: If you saw me standing by a pig what fruit would it remind you of?
KELLY: A pear.

Did you hear about the piglet who wasn't pretty and wasn't ugly?
She was pretty ugly.

What should you do if a wild boar charges through your front door?
Run out of the back door.

What do you call a pig after it's one year old?
A two-year-old.

When should you feed pig's milk to a baby?
When it's a baby pig.

What's the difference between a musician and a dead pig?
One composes, the other decomposes.

Where do pigs go in America?
New Pork.

What's pink, has four legs and flies?
A dead pig.

What should you do with a blue pig?
Try to cheer it up.

Why did the pigs go to live in the city?
They'd heard the country was at war.

Why aren't pigs any good at acting?
They're all old hams.

What are the best steps to take if you meet a wild boar?
Very big ones.

Where do good pigs go when they die?
To oven.

PIGLET: May I have a chemistry set for Christmas?
MOTHER PIG: What, and stink the sty out?

How do you stop a pig going oink on Monday morning?
Eat him for Sunday lunch.

What do you call a pig in a car park?
A porking lot attendant.

What do you get if you cross a pig with a hedgehog?
A pork-upine.

MOTHER: You shouldn't pull faces at that pig.
SAMANTHA: But he started it.

What did the pig win when it went on a successful diet?
The No-belly prize.

Why was the pig actor cross with his friend?
He kept hogging the stage.

PETER PIG: Would you like to come out tonight?
PRISCILLA PIG: No thanks, I'd rather sty at home.

Why is a pig in the bedroom
like a house on fire?
The sooner you put it out
the better.

Will the cows eat soup?
No, but the pigswill.

Why should you never steal a pig?
It might squeal to the police.

Did you hear about the lad who went to work on a pig
farm?
He complained that his work kept piling up.

Why can't pigs dance?
They have two left feet.

How do you stop a herd of pigs from charging?
Take away their credit cards.

Two pigs went to the zoo and stopped in front of the
hippos. 'What's that creature?' enquired little Petronella.
'It's a hippo,' said her mum.
'Fancy having to live with such an ugly face and that big,
fat body,' replied the little piglet.

A pig went into a café and ordered a chocolate milk shake. Thinking he would know nothing about money, the proprietor charged him £5. Then he added, to make conversation, 'We don't get many pigs in here.'

'With milk shakes costing £5 I'm not surprised,' replied the pig.

Why did the pig wear dark glasses? If you had all these jokes written about you, would you want to be recognised?

MAUREEN: Did you hear about the pig impersonator?
DOREEN: No. Did he make oink, oink noises?
MAUREEN: No, he did the smell.

BRIAN: My brother's got an appetite like a pig.
RYAN: And the figure to match.

PETER: I wish I had enough money to buy a Tamworth pig.
ANITA: What would you do with a Tamworth pig?
PETER: Nothing, I just wish I had that much money.

What looks like a pig but doesn't smell like a pig?
A photograph of a pig.

How do you know if a pig's in your bed?
By the letter P on his pyjamas.

Why are pigs pink?
So you can tell them apart from sheep.

What's pink and red all over?
An embarrassed pig.

What should you give a pig with diarrhoea?
Lots of room.

What does a pig do if it damages its trotters?
Gives up ballet dancing.

Where are pigs found?
They're so big and smelly they're not often lost.

What looks like a pig and flies?
A flying pig.

What would happen if pigs could fly?
Bacon would go up.

FATHER: Charlie! You're a pig! You know what a pig is, don't you?
CHARLIE: Yes, Dad, it's a hog's little boy.

ADAM: I've just bought a pig.
EVE: But where will you keep it?
ADAM: Under my bed.
EVE: But what about the smell?
ADAM: Oh, the pig will just have to get used to it.

Did you hear about
the pig called Biro?
That was just his
pen-name.

What do you call the story of the three little pigs?
A pigtail.

What did the vet do when the pig
got stuck in a chimney?
Gave him a flue jab.

Why did the pig buy three boxes
of paper hankies?
He had a stinking cold.

What do pigs do when they are let out into a field?
They aroma around.

What happens if a herd of wild pigs charges over Batman and Robin?
You get Flatman and Ribbon.

How do you get a porker in a matchbox?
Take the matches out first.

What did they call the pig who made two trips across the English Channel?
A dirty double-crosser.

DINER: Waiter, this ham is terrible.
WAITER: What makes you say that?
DINER: A little swallow told me.

How can you tell when a pig's
   been in your larder?
      It's empty!

Did you hear about the pig who sent his photo to a Lonely Hearts Club? They wrote back and said they weren't that lonely.

PAMELA PIG: I'm off to the beauty parlour.
PERCY PIG: I didn't know they could perform miracles.

When Pauline Pig went to the beauty parlour she was away for six hours. When she returned her friend Pattie looked hard at her and said, 'You've been away all this time and you don't look any different.'

'No,' said Pauline, 'I didn't have any treatment today, I just went for the estimate.'

PERRY PIG: I don't think this photo of me does me justice.
PADDY PIG: It's not justice you need, it's mercy.

Why is a pig smell like a remote control?
Because it turns everybody off.

Priscilla Pig went to a dance with her boyfriend Paul, and returned home in floods of tears. 'What did you do to upset her?' asked her angry mother.

'I don't know,' said Paul. 'I just paid her a compliment.'

'And what did you say?' persisted the mother.

'I told her she smelled less than any pig I'd ever danced with.'

PETRA PIG: The vet said I was overweight and should lose 10 kg. Whatever shall I do?
PIERS PIG: You could try cutting off your head.

'I wouldn't say Petra was overweight but if she were a human she could sit round a table all by herself.'

Mary had a little pig,
Her father shot it dead.
And now it goes to school
With her inside a roll of bread.

In which British town should you never buy a sandwich?
Oldham.

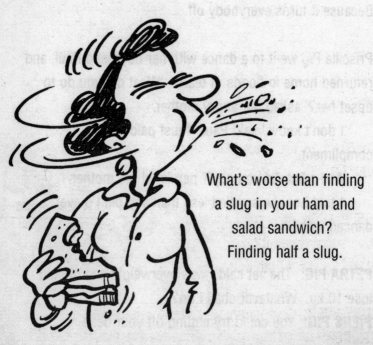

What's worse than finding
a slug in your ham and
salad sandwich?
Finding half a slug.

CUSTOMER: I'll have a ham and cockroach sandwich on brown bread, please.

DELICATESSEN MANAGER: Oh, I couldn't possibly serve you with anything like that.

CUSTOMER: Why not?

DELICATESSEN MANAGER: We're out of brown bread.

Two friends went into a cafe for lunch. Sally ordered a tongue sandwich. 'Ugh!' exclaimed her friend Susie. 'How can you eat something that's come out of a pig's mouth?'

'I hadn't thought of that,' said Sally. 'What are you going to have, then?'

'I'm having an egg sandwich,' replied Susie primly.

DINER: A pork steak and a glass of lemonade, please.

WAITER: Fillet?

DINER: Of course, to the top of the glass.

DINER: Why are there two worms on my plate?

WAITER: Those are your pork sausages, sir.

DINER: Why does my ham bun have scum round it?

WAITER: It's a Bath bun, sir.

DON'T EAT ME, I'VE GOT A RASHER

CUSTOMER: That ham you sold me was bad.

GROCER: It can't be, it was only cured last week.

Did you hear about the man who left all his money
to his pigs?
They were filthy rich.

What's the first thing a pig does in the morning?
Wakes up.

What do you call a pig with no legs?
It doesn't matter what you call him, he still won't come
when you do.

What's fat, pink and smelly and goes round and round?
A pig in a revolving door.
And what else?
A long-playing pig.

Why was the pig so small?
It was fed on
condensed milk.

Why do some pigs have Big Ears?
Because Noddy won't pay the ransom.

What goes oink, oink, oink, squelch, squelch, squelch?
A pig wearing wet plimsolls.

What's pink, has a curly tail,
goes oink and drinks blood?
A hampire.

Where was the pig when the lights went out?
In the dark.

PERCY PIG: My wife's beauty is timeless.
PADDY PIG: Do you mean her face could stop a clock?

What kind of pigs have their eyes closest together?
The smallest.

What kind of pigs can jump higher than a tree?
All kinds, trees can't jump.

Where would you find a pig's temple?
On the side of its head.

What do you call a pig lying in the gutter?
Dwayne.

What do you call a pig sitting on a bonfire?
Guy.

What do you call a pig who fell into the sea in a barrel?
Bob.

What's fat, pink and smelly and can see just as well from both ends?
A pig wearing a blindfold.

What's the best way to stop infection from pig bites?
Don't bite any pigs!

What happened to the pig who ran away with the circus?
The police made him bring it back.

Did you hear about the well-behaved piglet? When he was
good his mum gave him a penny and a pat on the head.
By the time he was two he had £20 in the bank and a
completely flat head.

PAMMY PIG: Will you still love me when I'm old and ugly?
PADDY PIG: Of course I do.

What do you call a female pig that climbs trees?
Ivy.

What do you call a pig that spends all its time lying
on the floor?
Matt.

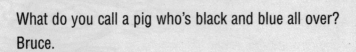

What do you call a pig who's black and blue all over?
Bruce.

Did you hear about the large pig who went on
a crash diet?
He wrecked two cars and a motorbike.

What's fat, pink and smelly and goes beep, beep?
A pig in a traffic jam.

What's fat, pink and smelly, goes beeeeep and overtakes
all the cars in front of it?
A road hog.

What's the difference between a sick pig and a dead bee?
One's a seedy beast; the other a bee deceased.

Did you hear the one about the three ham sandwiches?
No.
Two bad.

DINER: There's no ham in my
chicken and ham pie.
WAITER: There aren't
any shepherds in the shepherds'
pie, either, sir.

DINER: Why is there a button in my roast pork?
WAITER: It's from the jacket potato, sir.

ANDY: Do you prefer pork grilled or fried?
MANDY: Stop talking chop.

WAITER: What will you have to follow the roast pork?
MR RUMBLETUM: Indigestion, I expect.

A man walked into a pub with a dog on a lead. The landlord glowered at him and asked, 'What are you doing with that pig?'

Surprised, the man replied, 'It's not a pig, it's a dog.'

'Shut up,' snarled the landlord. 'I wasn't talking to you, I was talking to your dog.'

A man driving along a country lane ran over a pig as he passed a cottage. So he stopped the car, got out, knocked on the cottage door and apologised, saying, 'I'm so sorry for what happened, but I will replace your pig.'
'You flatter yourself,' replied the cottager.

ARCHIMEDES: Eureka!
MRS ARCHIMEDES: What of?
ARCHIMEDES: Pigs!

Knock, knock.
Who's there?
Saul.
Saul who?
Saul over your shoe, I can smell it from here.

'That piglet's spoiled, isn't it?'
'No, it's just the perfume it wears.'

How does a piglet tell if it's raining?
Sends his brother out of the sty and sees if he comes in wet.

VISITOR: Why do you call that pig food two-handed food?
FARMER: Because you feed it to them with one hand and hold your nose with the other.

How can you tell when there's a pig in the oven?
You can't shut the door.

VEGETARIANS FOR EVER

MRS ROUND: I always shop at Billy's, they have such lovely warm pork pies.

MRS LONG: That's because the cat sits on them all day.

FIRST PIG: I throw myself into everything I do.

SECOND PIG: Why don't you go and dig a big hole?

PIG TO PIGMAN: I've only got 50 seconds to live.

PIGMAN: Come here a minute.

A pig was walking down the road one day when she stopped another pig going in the same direction. 'Do I know you?' asked the second pig.

'Sorry,' answered the first. 'I thought I recognised you – your head looks just like my husband's behind.'

MOTHER PIG: What will you do when you're as big as your father?

PIGLET: Go on a diet.

FIRST PIG: Where do you bathe?

SECOND PIG: In the spring.

FIRST PIG: I said where, not when.

Little sparrow, flying high,
Dropped a message from the sky.
'Help!' said Andy, wiping his eye,
'What a blessing pigs can't fly!'

FIRST PIG: I was sorry to hear your head pigman had died. What was the complaint?
SECOND PIG: There haven't been any yet.

You can lead a pig to water, but you can't make him stink.

GERRY: What smells worse, a pig or your brother's socks?
KERRY: There's not a lot of difference.

SIGN IN A GROCER'S SHOP: Will customers please not sit on the bacon slicer as we are getting a little behind with our orders.

PIGMAN TO PIG: I never forget a face, but in your case I'll make an exception.

FARMER: Did you put the pigs out?
FARMER'S SON: Why, were they on fire again?

What would happen
if pigs could fly?
We'd need very large
umbrellas!

Why are pork sausages ill-mannered?
They spit in the frying-pan.

What did the pig say when the farmer grabbed him by the tail?
'This is the end of me.'

FIRST PIG: Oink, oink.

SECOND PIG: Moo, moo.

FIRST PIG: What do you mean, 'moo, moo'?

SECOND PIG: I'm learning a foreign language.

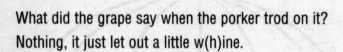

What did the grape say when the porker trod on it?
Nothing, it just let out a little w(h)ine.

What's brown, goes oink, and has a certain air about it?
A chocolate-covered pig.

What time is it when a pig climbs into your bed?
Time to change the sheets.

Why did Adam call a pig a pig?
Because it looked like a pig.

What's as fat as a pig but doesn't weigh anything?
His shadow.

What's a definition of will-power?
A pig going on a diet.

What's a definition of supreme will-power?
A pig staying on a diet.

How can you attract a pig?
Make a noise like an apple.

How does a pig get into an oak tree?
Sits on an acorn and waits for it to grow.

What's fat, green, and goes oink?
An unripe pig.

JACK: Would you rather a lion attacked you,
or a wild boar?
ZACK: I'd rather the lion attacked the wild boar.

How do you get down from a pig?
You don't get down from a pig, you get down from a swan.

Where do hogs keep their money?
In piggy banks.

What's the difference between a pig and an apple?
Pigs don't grow on trees.

What do you get if you cross a pig with a boy scout?
A pig that helps old ladies across the street.

What's the difference between a flea and a pig?
A pig can have fleas but a flea can't have pigs.

BILL: Did you know that, from a medical point of view, pigs are unique?
WILL: Really? Why?
BILL: Because first you kill them, then you cure them.

A policeman was treading his beat round the London streets when he found a man spreading powder everywhere. 'What are you doing?' he asked.

'I'm spreading powder, to keep pigs away,' explained the man.

'But there aren't any pigs in the middle of London,' said the surprised policeman.

'Exactly,' replied the man. 'It just shows how well this powder works.'

What's pink, goes oink and hops?
A pig on a pogo stick.

SIMON: That farmer's a magician.

SURESH: Why do you say that?

SIMON: He just told me he was going to turn his pigs into a field.

MICK: Did you hear the joke about the pigs?

NICK: No.

MICK: Never mind, it stinks.

FIRST PIG: How's your dinner?

SECOND PIG: It tastes swill.

Two old pigs, who had a philosophical outlook, were talking about the meaning of life. 'How can you be sure you exist?' asked one of the other.

'I stink, therefore I ham,' replied his friend.

What did the mother pig say to her piglets? 'Children should be smelled, not heard.'

Did you hear about the pig policeman who was promoted to be a detective? He joined the hamicide squad.

Did you hear about the high prices for pork? They've created a gold mine in the sty.

What do you get if you cross a pig with a boomerang? An awful smell you can't get rid of.

VISITING AUNT: And what do you want to be when you grow up?
PIGLET: A big stinker.

CAROL: My pig's got no nose.
DARRYL: How does he smell?
CAROL: Terrible.

Why do pigs eat so much?
They want to be hogs.

MOTHER: Keep that pig out of the house, it's covered in mud.
JIMMY: Keep out of the house, little piggy, it's covered in mud.

What do you get if you cross a pig with a young goat?
A dirty kid.

A mother pig had two piglets she called In and Out. One day, little In got lost, and they searched high and low for him. Eventually, just when it was getting dark and they'd almost given up hope, Out rushed in to the sty to say he'd been found. 'Wonderful!' exclaimed the mother pig. 'How did you manage to find him?'

'Oh, by In-stinked,' replied Out.

'My brother keeps pigs in the house and the smell is awful.'
'Couldn't you open a window?'
'What, and let all my pigeons out?'

FIRST PIG: I've heard that new shepard keeps very doubtful company.
SECOND PIG: Yes, the farmer told me he'd seen him with a crook!

When pigs have dinner, do they have a swill time?

Do pigs have meetings at a community scenter?

What has two legs, one wheel and stinks? A barrowload of pig manure.

43

FIRST PIG: If frozen water is iced water, what is frozen ink?

SECOND PIG: Iced ink.

FIRST PIG: You sure do!

PIGLET: Dad, there's a piglet in my class who says I look just like you.

DAD: And what do you say to him?

PIGLET: Nothing, he's bigger than me.

What are high-rise flats for pigs called?
Styscrapers.

What do pigs call their laundry?
Hogwash.

FIRST PIG: Do you always bathe in muddy water?

SECOND PIG: It wasn't muddy when I got in.

FIRST PIG: This swill tastes like bathwater.

SECOND PIG: How would you know?

JOHN: I've just been bitten by a pig.

DON: Did you put anything on it?

JOHN: No, he seemed to like it just as it was.

A small town near London had two butcher's shops which were great rivals. One butcher put up a sign saying, 'We sell our pork to the Queen.' The next day the other butcher had put up a sign, reading, 'God save the Queen.'

What's fat, pink, and goes
oink, oink, splat?
A pig falling off a cliff.

PERCY PIG: Is that perfume
I smell?

PATTIE PIG: It is, and you do.

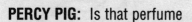

Why are pigs large and round and pink?
Because if they were small and white they'd be aspirins.

PEREGRINE PIG: I live on garlic alone.
PADDY PIG: Anyone who lives on garlic
should live alone.

What did the
absent-minded
pig say when the
wind changed direction?
'It's all coming back to me now.'

Did you know that today's pigs are tomorrow's bacon?

VISITOR: Why is that pig of yours giving me such a strange look?

FARMER: Probably because you're eating your strawberries out of his bowl.

What do you get if you cross a Persian carpet with a pig?
A large pile on the floor.

What do you get if you cross a zebra with a pig?
Striped sausages.

What do you do with a blue pig?
Sit it in front of the fire to warm it up.

What's the best way to catch a pig?
Chase it up into a tree and wait for the fall.

What's pink and white and goes up and down all day?
A ham sandwich in a lift attendant's pocket.

Why did the pig wear tartan braces?
To keep his tartan trousers up.

'Doctor, can you give me something for my liver?'
'Certainly, here's half a pound of bacon.'

FARMER: My pig's just swallowed a roll of film.
VET: Don't worry, nothing serious will develop.

'Why do you call your pig Carpenter?'
'Because he's always doing little jobs around the place.'

MOTHER PIG TO PIGLETS: Your father believes in energy conservation. He conserves all the energy he can.

JIM: My brother stopped a man from beating a pig.
TIM: It must have been a question of brotherly love.

KEV: We should take pigs at face value.
TREV: With faces like theirs that's not saying much!

A man was sitting in a pub with his pet pig when his friend came in with the evening paper and read out the football results. The pig remarked, 'Oh dear, Southampton lost again.' The man's friend looked surprised, but said nothing.

The following week the same thing happened. The friend read out the results, and the pig said, 'Oh dear, Southampton lost again.'

When the same thing happened on the third week, the man's friend asked, 'What does your pig say when Southampton wins?'

'I don't know,' replied the man. 'You see, I've only had him six months.'

GLEN: It says here that somewhere in the world a sow has piglets every 20 minutes.

GWEN: Someone should find her and stop her.

MOTHER PIG: Why is your brother crying?

PIGLET: Because I won't give him my bowl of food.

MOTHER PIG: But what about his own bowl of food?

PIGLET: He cried when I ate that, too.

JENNY: We had to have our pig put down.

BENNY: Was it mad?

JENNY: Well, it wasn't very happy.

How do you keep pigs from smelling?
Cut off their noses.

'That pig hasn't been himself recently.'
'I thought I'd noticed an improvement.'

PERCY PIG: My girlfriend's as pretty as a flower.
PADDY PIG: A cauliflower?

FIRST PIGLET: Our mum seems to be getting heavier.
SECOND PIGLET: Yes, I'd noticed her double chin had become a treble.

FIRST PIG: Looks aren't everything.
SECOND PIG: In your case they aren't anything.

'Pauline Pig has such a sympathetic face.'
'Yes, it has everyone's sympathy.'

'What do you think about Percy Pig's looks?'
'I don't mind him looking, it's his face I can't stand.'

POLLY PIG: I've just been on a crash diet.
MOLLY PIG: I thought you looked a wreck.

PHOEBE PIG: I'm the perfect shape.
PATTIE PIG: Yes, perfectly round.

Matthew and Mark were discussing a girl they knew. 'It's not that she's not pretty,' said Matthew, 'it's just that I feel that if I pulled her pigtail she'd probably go "oink oink".'

'Pigs aren't really bad looking.'
'No, they just have a little blemish between their ears – their faces.'

'How do you please a pig?'
'Tickle it under the chin.'
'Which chin?'

FARMER: I don't know why that pig's so fat, it eats like a bird.
FARMER'S WIFE: Yes, a vulture.

'Have you heard? Pauline Pig is watching her weight.'
'Yes, watching it go up.'

A piglet sat watching her mother cover her face in mud.
'What are you doing that for, Mum?' she asked.

'To make me beautiful,' her mother replied.

The piglet sat thoughtfully for a moment, and then said, 'But it doesn't work, does it?'

'That pig's so ugly that when a mosquito bites it it shuts its eyes.'

What did the pig say when he had only thistles to eat?
'Thistle have to do.'

'Those two piglets stick together.'
'If you were as dirty as they are you'd be sticky, too.'

What do you get if you cross an electric organ
with a hen?
Hammond eggs.

How does a pig
write a letter?
With a pen and oink.

Knock, knock.
Who's there?
Pigs.
Pigs who?
Pigs go oink, not who.

BERT: One of your pigs bit off my finger.
GERT: Which one?
BERT: I don't know, all pigs look alike to me.

TILLY: Can you spell 'blind pig'?
MILLY: B, L, I, N, D, P, I, G.
TILLY: No, that's not right, it's B, L, N, D, P, G. If it had
two eyes it wouldn't be blind.

Farmer Giles was praising his prize sow. 'She's one in a million,' he said.

His neighbour, Farmer Miles, sneered, 'Really? I thought she was won in a raffle.'

GEORGE: Why have you got a cold pork sausage stuck behind your ear?
JIM: Oh, dear, I must have eaten my pencil for lunch.

PATIENT: Doctor, everyone thinks I'm mad. You see, I love pork sausages.
DOCTOR: There's nothing mad about that. I like pork sausages, too.
PATIENT: You do? Then you must come round and see my collection. I've got hundreds.

Knock, knock.
Who's there?
Egon.
Egon who?
Egon a bacon roll.

DILLY: Do hams grow
on trees?
BILLY: No.
DILLY: Then what's an 'ambush?

Why did the pig cross the road?
It was the chicken's day off.

BRIAN: I've lost my pig.
BRENDA: Why don't you put an advertisement in the paper?
BRIAN: Don't be silly, he can't read.

How far can you chase a pig into a wood?
Only halfway – then you're chasing it out again.

BRIAN: What would happen if I stole that pig?
FATHER: You'd go to prison.
BRIAN: But you'd look after her for me while I was away, wouldn't you?

If you shoot a pink pig with a pink gun, what do you shoot a black pig with?
A black gun?
No, you paint the pig pink and shoot it with the pink gun.

A farmer was showing a schoolboy round his pig farm. 'How many pigs do you reckon there are?' he asked.

The boy thought for a moment. 'Two hundred and eighty-four,' he replied.

The farrmer was impressed. 'That's very clever,' he said. 'How did you manage to count them so quickly?'

'Oh, it was simple,' replied the lad. 'I just counted all the legs and divided by four.'

HERBERT: Any pig must have three tails.

HAROLD: That's silly, of course it hasn't.

HERBERT: Look at it this way. Any pig has more tails than no pig, right?

HAROLD: Ye-es.

HERBERT: And no pig has two tails, right?

HAROLD: Yes.

HERBERT: So any pig must have three tails.

ART TEACHER: What have you drawn, Polly?

POLLY: A pig eating acorns, Miss.

ART TEACHER: But where are the acorns?

POLLY: The pig's eaten them all.

ART TEACHER: And where is the pig?

POLLY: Well, after he'd eaten all the acorns he went off to look for more food.

MR ROUNDTUM: We had roast boar for dinner last night.

MR REDFACE: Was it a wild boar?

MR ROUNDTUM: Well, it wasn't very pleased.

Mr and Mrs Bollard were on a safari holiday when they encountered a herd of wild boar. The pigs turned, and charged at Mr Bollard. In desperation he shouted at his wife, who was carrying all the equipment, 'Shoot, Edna, shoot!'

'I can't do that,' she called back.

'Why not?' he yelled.

'Because I've run out of film.'

Farmer Brown took his prize pig to the vet because it had injured a trotter. The vet examined it, then shook his head sadly. 'I'm afraid it will never be right,' he said.

'Why not?' asked the farmer.

'Because it's on his left leg,' replied the vet.

GILLY: My sister prepared our supper last night. We had cold boiled ham.

MILLY: Was it good?

GILLY: No, she boiled it in cold water.

WAITER: How did you find your pork chop, sir?

DINER: Oh, I just lifted a chip and there it was.

PRISCILLA PIG: Tara the Tamworth pig is so silly. She can't see further than the nose on her face.

PAULA PIG: True, but with her nose that's quite a distance.

Did you hear about the two pigs who met in a revolving door? They're still going round together.

What's fat, pink and smelly and goes round and round? A pig in a revolving door.

MRS BROWN: That pork is a bargain.

MRS WHITE: Really?

MRS BROWN: Yes, 50% is off.

What would you do if a very large pig sat in front of you at the cinema?
Miss most of the film.

Can you kill a pig by throwing eggs at it?
Yes, you can eggs-terminate it.

Did you hear about the Vietnamese pot-bellied pig mother whose piglets were so ugly she didn't push their pram, she pulled it?

What was proved when the porker was run over by the steam roller?
That he had a lot of guts.

Why are pigs pink?
So they can hide in strawberry patches.

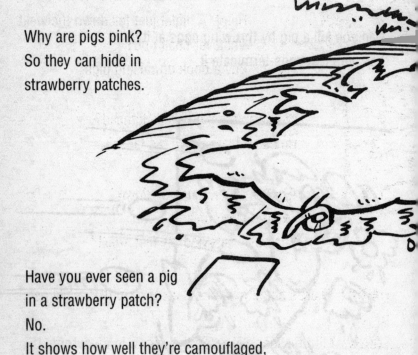

Have you ever seen a pig in a strawberry patch?
No.
It shows how well they're camouflaged, doesn't it?

'Waiter, this food isn't fit for a pig to eat!'
'Wait a moment, sir, and I'll bring you some that is.'

FIRST PIG: You've got an awful-looking thing on your neck.
SECOND PIG: Oh, dear, what is it?
FIRST PIG: Your head.

SIGN IN A DELICATESSEN:

Our tongue sandwiches speak for themselves.

'Help! A piglet just fell down the well!
Whatever shall I do?'
'Buy a book on raising pigs.'

Why was the pig called Hothead?
He had a blaze down his face.

'That pig is built upside down.'
'What do you mean?'
'His nose runs and his feet smell.'

HARRY: There's something about a pig farm that really gets to you.
LARRY: Mmm, especially when the wind's in the wrong direction.

PERCIVAL PIG: What's your perfume called?
PEONY PIG: 'High Heaven'.
PERCIVAL PIG: It certainly stinks to it.

What did the pig say when the bull charged it?
Nothing, pigs can't talk.

SUSIE: Are we having Aunt Ida for Sunday lunch?
MOTHER: No, dear, roast pork as usual.

Why does a pig take a hammer to bed?
So he can hit the hay.

A man was driving along a country lane past a farm when his car broke down. He got out and lifted up the bonnnet to see if he could discover what was the matter, when he heard a voice from the other side of the hedge saying, 'Check the spark plugs.' So he looked over the hedge, and there was a large black pig. 'Why don't you check the spark plugs,' it repeated.

Astonished, the man went up to the farmhouse, where he met the farmer and told him what had happened. 'Was it a black pig?' asked the farmer.

The man nodded. 'Then take no notice of him. Black pigs don't know anything about cars.'

What did the cobbler say when a pig wandered into his shop?
'Shoo!'

What is pigskin most used for?
Holding pigs together.

What do you get if you cross a pig with a bad driver?
A crashing boar.

FIRST PIGLET: When's your birthday?
SECOND PIGLET: 19 March.
FIRST PIGLET: Which year?
SECOND PIGLET: Every year.

FIRST PIGLET: I think I've just swallowed a bone.
SECOND PIGLET: Are you choking?
FIRST PIGLET: No, I'm serious.

What two things should a pig never eat before breakfast?
Lunch and supper.

MINISTRY OFFICIAL: How many people work on this pig farm?
FARMER: About half of them.

One of the most popular attractions at a travelling fair was
a pig that played the piano. A tourist who saw it could
hardly believe his eyes, and went to find the animal's trainer
afterwards. 'Your pig is absolutely amazing,' he said.
    'Not really,' replied the trainer. 'He took lessons for years.'

If a pig broke its leg in two places, what should it do?
Stay away from those places in future.

Why is a pig halfway through a hedge like a coin?
Because he has a head on one side and a tail on the other.

Two farmers were attending a farm sale. 'Find any bargains?' asked the first.

'Aye,' replied the second. 'I bought a pigsty in mint condition.'

'You mean it was as good as new?' asked the first.

'No,' answered his friend. 'It had a hole in the middle.'

Where did the pig go after his sixth year?
Into his seventh.

TEACHER: Name five farm animals for me, Darren.
DARREN: Er, a cow, a sheep . . . and three pigs.

Which pig has the biggest trotters?
The pig with the biggest feet.

What's the best thing to feed to racing pigs?
Runner beans.

PIGLET: But I don't want to go to America, Mum.
MOTHER: Shut up and keep swimming.

What's the best day to eat bacon?
Fry-day.

Why don't bald pigs use keys?
They don't have any locks.

How do you stop a pig squealing in the back of a car?
Put him in the front.

Two hunters discovered wild boar tracks in the forest.
The first looked around nervously, as if expecting a herd
of them to come and charge him at any minute.

'Shall we follow them?' asked his friend.

'Tell you what,' the friend replied. 'You see where
they're going and I'll go back to try and see where they
came from.'

A boy pig sent the following verse to a girl pig on Valentine's Day:
The rain makes all things beautiful,
The grass and flowers too.
If rain makes all things beautiful,
Why doesn't it rain on you?

Where is a Vietnamese pot-bellied pig beautiful?
In the dark.

What did the pig say to the tree root?
'It's been nice gnawing you.'

Why did the pig put his bed in the fireplace?
He wanted to sleep like a log.

What did the pig say when all he was given to eat was a beetroot?
'This beets all.'

BLONDE PIGS HAVE MORE FUN

PETER PIG: May I see you pretty soon?
PAULA PIG: Don't you think I'm pretty now?

Are pigs pretty?
Put it this way, if you held a beauty contest, no one would win.

PATTIE PIG: My husband calls me the best looker in the world.

PETRA PIG: My husband has poor eyesight, too.

PEREGRINE PIG: Do you think I'll lose my looks as I get older?

PERCIVAL PIG: With any luck, yes.

PEONY PIG: I've just come back from the beauty parlour.

PAULINE PIG: Too bad they were closed.

Mr Mudd the pig farmer always remembers his wife's birthday. It's the day after she reminds him about it.

MR MUDD: And why are you late this morning, Jimmy?

JIMMY SLUDGE: I'm not really late, boss, I just took my tea break before coming to work.

Mr Mudd was interviewing for a new pigman. 'Can you handle a variety of work?' he asked one candidate.

'I should be able to,' answered the lad, 'I've had 20 jobs in three months.'

FIRST PIGLET: A funny thing happened to my mother in Wiltshire.

SECOND PIGLET: I thought you were born in Norfolk.

MIKE: Some say pigs can talk.

SPIKE: It's not true. If you meet a pig who says he can talk, he's lying.

TRACEY: But I met a pig who could talk and do mental arithmetic.

STACEY: What happened?

TRACEY: I asked it what 5 minus 5 was and it said nothing.

CHARLIE: I play chess with my pig.

CECIL: He must be very clever.

CHARLIE: Not really. I win most games.

On which side do pigs have the most whiskers?
The outside.

Did you hear about the pig farmer who decided to try something new? He sold his pig farm and bought another 10 kilometres long and 1 metre wide. He says he's going to grow spaghetti.

SALESMAN: These new pigsties come with a five-year guarantee, provided you don't put pigs in them.

FARMER BROWN: Is your prize sow old?
FARMER BLACK: She's approaching middle age, for the third time.

How do you describe an old pig?
When he walks he creaks and when he talks he squeaks.

Why did the farmer wash his pig in a square bathtub?
So he wouldn't leave a ring.

A PIG IS FOR LIFE... NOT JUST CHRISTMAS

Did you hear about the piglet who was born on 24 December?
He wanted to be home for Christmas.

Mrs Broadbeam, who was very large, was visiting Sharon's mother. 'Could you get down on your hands and knees, please?' asked Sharon.

'Whatever for?' asked Mrs Broadbeam.

'Our teacher says we've got to draw a pig for our homework.'

NOTICE IN A BUTCHER'S SHOP:
John Smith butchers pigs like his father.

Where was bacon first fried?
In Greece.

What do you get if you cross a pig with a lion?
Sausages that eat you.

Why did the pig wear red trousers?
His blue ones were in the wash.

What's pink, goes oink and climbs trees?
A pig. (I lied about it climbing trees).

What's pink and blue, goes oink and climbs trees?
A pig wearing jeans. (I'm still lying about it climbing trees).

DAVE: Do you say a pig's trotters is blue or a pig's trotters are blue?
MAVE: Neither, a pig's trotters are pink!

Which takes more chances, a beef steak or a slice of bacon?
A slice of bacon, because it's a little rasher.

How do you take a sick pig to hospital?
In a hambulance.

JANICE: Six pigs stood under an umbrella and none got wet. How come?

JENNY: It was a giant umbrella?

JANICE: No, it wasn't raining!

SALLY: Why do you call your pig 'Ben Hur'?

WALLY: Well, he was just called Ben until she had piglets!

FIRST PIG, LOOKING AT THE SKY: I'd hate to be up there in a plane.

SECOND PIG: I'd hate to be up there without one.

Why wouldn't the pig farmer travel by plane?

Because the journey to the airport made him carsick.

The pig farmer was interviewing lads to come and work on the farm. 'Do you like hard work?' he asked one.

'No, sir,' he replied.

'You're hired,' said the farmer. 'That's the first honest answer I've heard today.'

FIRST BOAR: How's your new family?

SECOND BOAR: Oh, fine. They said the piglets looked like me, then they turned them the right way up.

FIRST PIG: She's the ugliest pig I ever saw.
SECOND PIG: My dear, you forget yourself.

What music could the pigs hear in their field?
Popcorn.

How can a pig cover a chair?
By sitting on it.

If 12 pigs make a dozen, how many make a million?
Very few!

Why is a pig smell very obedient?
Because it's scent wherever it goes.

STAN: What's the difference between a pig and a pillarbox?
JAN: I don't know.
STAN: I shan't send you to post my letters then.

75

CUSTOMER: That joint of pork you sold me last week was awful.

BUTCHER: Was it tough?

CUSTOMER: Tough? I couldn't even get my fork into the gravy.

BILL: Do you like my new cap?

BEN: Yes, but what happened to your pork-pie hat?

BILL: The gravy kept running down my ears.

Farmer Brown fed his pigs on potatoes, but when he went to buy his supplies he complained that the previous lot he'd bought had been full of eyes. 'Well,' replied the merchant, 'you did ask for enough to see you through the winter.'

If it takes a football team 45 minutes to eat a ham, how long will it take three football teams to eat half a ham? It depends whether they are professionals or 'am-a-chewers.

A mother pig caught one of her piglets in the feed store. 'What are you up to?' she asked.

'I'm up to my sixth apple,' replied the piglet, 'but they were only little ones.'

PIGLET TO DAD: I bet there's something I can do that you can't do.

DAD: What's that?

PIGLET: Grow up.

MOTHER PIG: No, you can't have any more food, it's bad for you to sleep on a full stomach.

PIGLET: I can lie on my side.

Adam was naming the animals. 'And that,' he said, ' is a pig.'

'Why do you call it a pig?' asked Eve.

'Because it looks like a pig, silly,' replied Adam.

DINER: I'll have a lamb chop. No, make that a pork chop.

WAITER: I'm not a magician, sir.

DINER: The soup, please, followed by the roast pork.

WAITER: If I were you, sir, I'd have the pork first, it's on the turn.

DINER: How long will my pork sausages be?

WAITER: Oh, about 6 or 8 centimetres.

DINER: I asked for bread with my dinner.
WAITER: It's in the pork sausages, sir.

DINER: Why have you served my roast pork in a nosebag?
WAITER: The head waiter says you eat like a horse, sir.

DINER: Two pork chops, please, and make them lean.
WAITER: Certainly, sir, which way?

What did the tomato say to the ham?
'You go on ahead and I'll ketchup.'

Why do pigs wear wellies?
To keep their feet dry in the mud.

Farmer Brown met Farmer Green wandering around his fields. 'What are you looking for?' he asked.

'A pig with one eye called Mildred,' replied Farmer Green.

'What's her other eye called?' asked Farmer Brown.

TEACHER: Can you correct this sentence, children, 'The boar and the sow was in the field'.
NELLY: It should be, 'The sow and the boar was in the field', Miss.
TEACHER: Why do you say that, Nelly?
NELLY: You should always put ladies first, Miss.

Where do Californian pigs go dancing?
San Frandisco.

Two girl piglets were talking about a friend of theirs.
'The boys don't call her pretty and they don't call her ugly,' said one.

'No, they just don't call her,' agreed the other.

CUSTOMER: Have you got a pig's head?
BUTCHER: No, it's just the way I part my hair.

A farmer was taking on a lad to help with the pigs. 'You realise we work very early hours?' he said.

'Yes,' said the lad.

'And you don't mind?'

'No,' he replied. 'I don't mind how early I go home.'

JOHNNY: Hey, your piglet has just bitten my ankle!
RONNIE: That's because he's not big enough to bite your neck.

What do they call little black pigs in Russia?
Black piglets.

Knock, knock.
Who's there?
Trotter.
Trotter who?
Trotter down the road for me.

Knock, knock.
Who's there?
Arthur.
Arthur who?
Arthur any pigs on your farm?

Knock, knock.
Who's there?
Police.
Police who?
Police let me see the piglets.

How can you stop a ham sandwich from going bad?
Eat it.

DINER: Take this pork chop away! I've been trying to cut it for 10 minutes and it's so tough my knife has made no impression at all.
WAITER: I'm afraid I can't do that, sir.
DINER: Why not?
WAITER: You've bent it.

Why did the butcher put pennies in the pork pies?
He'd been asked for some change in the recipe.

'Why aren't you eating your gammon steak?'
'I'm waiting for the mustard to cool.'

What game do pigs play in a matchbox?
Squash.

What's pink and yellow, pink and yellow, pink and yellow?
A pig rolling down a hill with a bunch of daffodils in its
mouth.

'Why's your pig called Ink?'
'Because he ran out of the pen.'

What do you get if you cross a bell with a pig?
Something that peals and squeals.

What do you do with a pig with a broken toe?
Ring for a tow truck.

DINER: Will my ham omelette be long?
WAITER: No, sir, round.

Why did the mother pig call two of her piglets Edward?
Because two Eds are better than one.

What do you call a pig who lives
in the biggest city in America?
A New Yorker porker.

What do you need to know
to teach a pig tricks?
More than the pig!

FIRST FARMER: My pig died of flu.

SECOND FARMER: I didn't know pigs caught flu.

FIRST FARMER: This one flew under the tractor.

FARMER AT MARKET: I like this pig, but his legs are too short.

PIG DEALER: They do all reach the floor, sir.

MOTHER: Don't pull the pig's tail!

MILLY: It's him that's doing the pulling.

What do you get if you cross a pig with a locomotive? Something that grunts and shunts.

A boy took his pet pig to the cinema. It sat quietly beside him and appeared to enjoy the film. As they were leaving, the usherette said, 'Isn't it amazing that your pig should enjoy the film?'

'It is rather,' agreed the lad. 'He didn't like the book at all.'

What would you get if you fed a pig on £5 notes?
Rich pork.

FIRST FARMER: I paid £100 for that creature – it's part pig and part bull.
SECOND FARMER: Which part's the bull?
FIRST FARMER: The part about the £100!

MOTHER PIG: How many times must I tell you not to fight? You must learn to give and take!
PIGLET: But I did, Mum. I gave him a bite on the nose and took his apple.

GIRL PIGLET: Females are cleverer than males, you know.
BOY PIGLET: Really? I never knew that!
GIRL PIGLET: See what I mean?

GIRL PIGLET: That young boar's annoying me.

HER FRIEND: But he's not even looking at you.

GIRL PIGLET: I know, that's what's annoying me.

If a mother pig had eight daughters and each daughter
had a brother, how many piglets did she have?
Nine - the son is each daughter's brother.

VISITOR: What are your new piglets' names?

FARMER: I don't know, they won't tell me.

JENNY: What's your favourite animal?

KENNY: A pig.

JENNY: And what's your favourite colour?

KENNY: Green.

JENNY: And what's your favourite number?

KENNY: Eight. Why?

JENNY: Have you ever seen an eight-legged green pig?

What should you do with a green pig?
Send it to school.

Why do pigs read dirty magazines?
They always drop them on the floor.

Why did the old pig go on a diet?
Because he was thick to his stomach.

What do seven days of dieting do to a pig?
They make one weak.

FIRST PIG: Have you had your breakfast yet?
SECOND PIG: Yes, I was so hungry at 7.50 that I 8 o'clock.

What did the pig have for his breakfast in bed?
A few rolls and a turnover.

VISITOR: Why has your pig got a wooden leg?
FARMER: Because it saved my life.
VISITOR: How?
FARMER: One night, the farmhouse caught fire and it rang the Fire Brigade.
VISITOR: But how did that give it a wooden leg?
FARMER: You don't think that I'd eat ALL of such a wonderful pig, do you?

What's it called when a farmer takes his pigs in a trailer to market?
Squeals on wheels.

Who wrote *Why I Went to Market*?
Tobias A. Pigg.

Who wrote *Let's Go to Market*?
Hugo First.

Who wrote *The Pigs that Got Away*?
Gay Topen

BRIAN: I heard a new pig joke yesterday. Did I tell it to you?

BERTIE: Is it funny?

BRIAN: Yes.

BERTIE: Then you didn't.

What did the pig say when he went to market?
'Armageddon out of here!'

Who wrote *The Ugly Old Pig*?
Ida Face.

What's the quickest way to increase the size of your pigs?
Look at them through a telescope

FATHER PIG: You've been going round telling everybody I'm a bore!

MOTHER PIG: I'm sorry, I didn't think it was a secret!

What's black and white and very noisy?
A saddleback playing the bagpipes.

What's pink, goes oink and spins round and round?
A pig in a washing machine.

Do pigs get up early?
Yes, at the crackling of dawn.

What do pigs have that no other animal has?
Piglets.

A farmer was interviewing a young man who wanted to come and work on his farm. 'And are you fit and healthy, and not prone to having accidents?' He asked.

'Oh, yes,' relied the lad.
'Then why are you walking on crutches?' asked the farmer. 'You seem to have had an accident already?

'Oh, that,' answered the lad. 'That happened at my last job. The boar charged me and knocked me over, but it was no accident, he did it on purpose.'

MOTHER PIG: You just wait until I find out who gave you that black eye!
PIGLET: No one gave it to me, Mum, I had to fight for it!

JACK: Did you hear my last pig joke?
ZACK: I certainly hope so!

THE END